PIERCING SHRIEKS

By
William Armstrong

Terror poetry and a one-act play, <u>The Hound,</u> based on a
short story by H.P. Lovecraft

Wrong Place, Wrong Time

I had stopped my car outside
The pounding rain a danger
Lightening meant the storm would rage
And make my hope of sleep a stranger

Thunder sounded dread drum beats
My soul retreated every blast
From the car to the bar
Each lightening flash a white-hot scar
I prayed the torrent quickly past

The bar was warm and quiet
No music did I hear
No-one spoke a single word
Their staring eyes made me feel drear

The room was old and dingy
The floor was scuffed and worn
The bar stools rubbed from many seats
The faded wallpaper, ripped and torn

There were photos on the walls
Of people long ago
Their faces could be barely seen
The grimy frames were want to show

And of the people staring
One dozen silent looked
Some had drinks, others food
Some were sitting, others stood
And one was writing in a book

Behind the bar, a woman leaned
Young and fresh and clean
But something told, she was quite old
The ancient style of her clothing

"Hello, sir, my name is 'Trish
My father owns this place
I can make any drink you like."
A smirk crept across her face

"Some food, young lady, is fine.
I missed my dinner tonight."
She pointed where a table and chair
Sat waiting for me to alight

I sat and stared in wonder,
At the plate that was already there.
Meat and potatoes, a glass of beer,
Exactly my favorite kind of fare.

My stomach growled in hunger
So I dug in with gluttony dour
The food was perfect, delicious and hot
My fork was a blur for at least an hour

'Trish was soon at my side
She set down another full plate
I could not stop, like a pig before slop
My growing hunger would not abate

A fear began deep inside me
As 'Trish came over once again
I never had eaten so much all at once
"You merely have to say 'When'".

"That's all for now, 'Trish, thank you."
With a frown, she walked to the bar
The patrons all scowled, then whispered aloud
"Ungrateful young man, to your car."

But, my legs were suddenly weak
A dizziness filled my head
I stood to leave and almost fell
My body trembled in dread

Was I poisoned? I wondered frightened
Were these people killing me here?
Would I die in the midst of a thunder storm
Far from friends and family dear?

But death was not in my future
As I found out later that night
My eyelids drooped, my shoulders stooped
I felt robbed of all of my might

Suddenly, standing beside me
Was another woman, a vision sublime
Jet-black hair, snow-white skin
Her tattooed face, all spider web lines

A face of alabaster,
Eyes shone midnight black
Dandelions in her hair
A tangled, silken stack

Her blood-red lipstick shined too bright
And called me to her kiss
Those satin lips gave me a smile
Like tickles from razor fingertips

She knew she had me in her grasp

Her gaze said 'You are mine.'
Her feet moved slowly, step by step
My desire would last a long, long time

Slowly, slow as syrup sweet
Her arms encircled 'round me
Drawing me, longing, into a dance
An aching sway, a misted trance
Her arms meant she'd never set me free

"I'm Ildia, come with me now
I have a place for your rest."
On trembling legs, I moved to her side
"The room I'm giving you is our best."

I followed her up some stairs
They creaked loudly with years
Our footsteps sounded
With each, my heart pounded
And increased my deepening fears

"This is the room, my sweet."
Ildia opened the door with a grin
The air was musty, dry and dusty
Bugs skittered gone 'cross the floor

The bed was like a magnet
It drew my fatigue to lie down
My common-sense screamed, to fast run away
But Idia's perfume tranced me to stay
As she reached for the buttons of her gown

We lay down on soft, satin pillows
Silken sheets caressing our skin
And soon and away, my body found sleep
But there was no rest from the fires within

Our passion was played out in flames
I felt I was falling for days
The air around us was frigid and stale
She shrieked in answer to my terrorized impale
And tore my soul in a thousand ways

I awoke all alone, drenched in sweat
And dressed, tears soaking my face
I had to leave, my life was believe
That my doom was coming apace

So, from the building I bolted
And through the storm, I ran
My car was waiting, I slammed on the gas
And flew from that nightmare without a plan

Four hours later, I stopped
And skidded to a halt' neath a tree
Its branches stretched for endless miles
But gave me no shelter
From the storm that pounded me

I lay down and slept once more
And dreamed of the bar and her face
But, something was wrong,
It seemed too real
Like a memory bought of disgrace

Then, I opened my eyes
And screamed till my throat was torn
For, staring down at my sweat-bathed body
Was Ildia, back in the bed, old and worn

"My love, never again try to leave me."
Instead of a smile, there was nothing but
hate
And furious loathing covered her face
And of her beauty, there was not a trace
"We stand now together at forever's gate."

"I chose you among all the others."
Her breath was a fetid repulse
"You are mine, for eternity's length.
You agreed with our first carnal kiss."

Now, the years trudge silently past
And to Ildia, I'm eternally wed
Our room is my tomb, my haven and home
My soul is her toy, our bed deathly joy
Where we share the kiss of the dead

Chinese New Fear

"Light the candle, my love,
Let the lantern float on its way."
The river was full of paper boats
Each one with a wish for the day

We were visiting China
And enjoying the fun of New Year
The colorful dragons and painted faces
And kimonos sewn silken with cheer

Thousands were out to enjoy
The evenings' fun and good food
Candles gave off soft, golden light

Music and dancing enhanced the mood

Smiles were all around us
And cheering with clapping after
We smelled the smoke and heard the
shouting
And we joined in the joyous laughter

"Make a wish with your eyes closed
And keep them that way 'til it's gone."
We held hands and made our wish
As the lantern floated to eternities' song

"So, what did you wish for, my sweet?"
I held her as close as I could
"I can't tell you that, or it won't come true."
I hugged her and suggested we go get some
food

Suddenly on the water,
Where our lantern had floated away,
An explosion sounded, like a boom from a
cannon
And a flash turned the night into day

Everyone screamed and shouted
As food stalls shook and collapsed
An acrid fog rolled into sight
No-one smiled or laughed

The river began to boil
Waves rose and pounded the shore
Lightening flashed from a clear sky

Burning heat blasted the air
Our amazing evening was no more

We looked at all the others
The partiers running around
Some just stared in dread and fear
Others were cowering, covering their head
While many lay still on the ground

Then, of a sudden, a roar
Throaty and angry and deep,
Shook the air with waves of terror
A nightmare sound, though none were
asleep

And then, it rose, slow and strong
And looked towards the shore where we
stood
A terrible form, all hatred and teeth
A mountain that moved in the moon

And so, we stood in terror
And stared at the form of our death
Its face was round and flattened
Its body was long and glistened
Our disbelief robbed us of breath

It was as long as a freight train
And moved, fluid and sleek
Its scales were silver, green and gold
Its eyes were red, fiery and old
Its smell was the sewer's reek

It came on like a ton of fury
Its shriek split the air into two
We turned and ran into nearby hills
Then stopped to see what it would do

What came next was horror
Our minds broke at what we saw
The beast crouched low and started to feed
It shredded and tore with its maw

It ate the people who lie there
Blood flowed like water, and soon
Nothing was left of our friends at the party
The sight made us weak and we swooned

Then, it sniffed the air
And looked where we were hid
It started to move at us without seeing
We sensed our doom and were sick

So, now we cower in fear
As this thing thunders closers by steps
There's nowhere to run
No escape from our fate
From looming and shrieking red death

Turnabout

"A Ouija board. How cliché.
Come on, Sheila. Let's jet."
"No, Bryan," she said, her face turning red.
"I'm not ready to leave just yet."

"But, this spirit board is different.
It doesn't call fiends from below."
The white-haired seer smiled as she spoke
"The answers come from a place pure as
snow."

"There are five of here tonight," she said,
"We all come seeking truth.
You're wealthy and beautiful, handsome and
fun
And everyone envies your youth."

"Now, all of us sit 'round this table
And everyone touch the planchette.
And make sure you notice
It's shaped like a teardrop,
I'll explain in a minute, but not just yet."

"Close your eyes and be quiet.
We have to be calm and serene.
We'll see some sights, none will give
frights.
There'll be nothing to cause you to scream."

"This is lame," Dale complained "let's
forget it.
Let's leave, Pam, and go out to drink."
"No, let go, I'm staying right here.
If you don't like it just go away."

"I agree, Sheila, let's take off now.
We can drive to a party near here."
"You can drive yourself, you weird creep.

We're done. Our relationship puts me to
sleep."
And, with that, he burst into tears

"That's enough. All of you must be silent.
Let's start. You'll like what you see.
With a bored sigh, they all closed their eyes
"Can you hear? It now has begun."

Without having asked any questions
A breeze, cool, fresh and alive
Blew through the room and made them all
gasp
Each and every one answered with a smile

"Yes, this is just what I wanted,
To show you a place you will love.
Now, open your eyes and see for yourselves
All the beauty, below and above."

With a shout, all at once, they gazed
At a vista, breathtaking and vast
Snow-covered mountains, a lake-centered
meadow
And a majesty their souls could not grasp

"You're joking, aren't you? This is fake."
Dale's voice was hardly a whisper
"It's as real as it seems, the trees and the
streams."
Then, she pointed to a castle sunk in mist

Snow began falling very lightly

It fell on their cheeks just like tears
And, as they stood, the soft breeze, it grew
As they watched, the mist moved slowly
near

A roar soundly loud in the distance
The mist turned thick and cold
The snowflakes fell, and grew in size
Something was wrong, they needn't be told

The roaring sound grew ever closer
Adrenaline pounded their bodies
They wanted to run, but could not see where
As the snow fell in increasing eddies

"What's going on? What's wrong?"
Was the question all of them asked
"I lied to you all, Hell itself beckons loud,
And to see you there, I have been tasked."

"All of you face endless suffering.
Your choices in life have been bad.
You've killed and lied, you've played with
lives
And a wonderful time you have had."

"I've killed no-one," Pam cried, as the wind
rose.
"But, you brought a man to his ruin.
You claimed his love, his money, his house.
He lost it all; suicide was his doom."

"I haven't caused anyone's death," Dale
yelled,
To be heard over the rising wind
"But, your anger and jealousy, fury and fists
Put a man in a coma, and he never awoke.
You're here to pay for your deathly sin.

"I'm innocent of mortal wasting,"
Sheila screamed, her tears hard as ice
"Another looked at your man with lust,
You hated her beauty and voluptuous form,
So you hired a man to commit deadly vice."

Bryan stood still and silent
He knew he was where he belonged
"And last of all, he's the worst of you,
The discordant note in my vengeance song."

"But, why should he be here," Pam shrieked,
She looked Bryan in dismay
"My brother is gentle, quiet and nice.
He wouldn't do anything harmful, I say."

"Should you tell your sister, or I?"
Bryan stared at his feet and was still
"Your brother's the one the newspapers call
'The Chemist' who poisons whole families
gone
It is sixteen poor souls he has killed

"He finds a house which is empty
And enters the place late at night
Then, he uses a rat poison, poured into food

To cause pain and bleeding and stop their
hearts tight."

The wind, then, rose to a shriek.
The snow turned to glass with an edge.
Each flake, when it struck, cut and stuck
And tore at their tender, young flesh.

Chunks of skin fell asunder.
Eyes were quickly made blind.
Clothes were shredded, muscles were
flayed.
Their throat-tearing screams were lost in the
wind.

"Before I leave, understand,
This all is perfectly just and right.
You used other people as innocent pawns,
But, there's always a price to pay for your
might."

And with those words, she was gone,
And left them screaming in pain.
An echo then whispered inside of their
brains,
"Maybe someday I'll come and free you
again."

They wander, forever, in agony,
In a snowstorm, eternally lost.
Each has died a thousand times
And come back to suffer in snow-choked
climes,

An example of violent humanities' cost.

Photoevil

The town was old, the people worn,
Paint was peeling, clothes were faded.
I stopped my car, killed the engine,
Beside a park, green and shaded.

Fall had come with its festivals.
Everywhere were decorations.
Paper witches and jack-o-lanterns.
Inky ghosts howled lamentations.

I stepped outside and closed the door
The air was warm and quiet
The town was not what I was used to
There was a charm, I could not deny it

I stepped into a diner there
The door slapped closed behind me
A waitress sat me down and asked
"What would you like to eat?"

I looked around the tidy place
Crammed from ceiling to floor
With photos, nic-nacs and various things
A jumble of attic and basement décor

Then my eyes beheld a sight
A photograph, old and dusty
It showed a photo of a young woman

Pale and beautiful and busty

Her smile was bright and cheery
Her eyes were laughing, too
Her hair was long and braided
She looked to be about twenty-two

I asked the waitress who she was
"She's dead, that's all I'll say
She wasn't loved by the town.
In fact, she's hated to this day."

But, as I ate my food and stared
Into the girl's round face
I began to feel excited and panicked
I started to sweat, my heart to race

I found myself moving closer
To the wall where the picture hung
And as I stared at her flowing hair
My heart burned as if it were stung

"You shouldn't sit so close,"
The waitress called out to me
"That girl was bad, some would say evil."
"I simply moved closer so I could see."

"Lots of men want that picture,
Since they can't have the girl in the frame.
She used to cause to cause the men in this
town
To fight over her, their passions inflamed"

"What is her name?" I whispered
I was barely able to speak
I couldn't move off of the chair
My body was shaking and weak

"Marilyn Hask was her maiden name
She married four times, over all.
And every man she saw and wanted
Started out rich and gave her all."

"Two of her husbands killed themselves,
The fourth one shot the third,
To clear the way to claim her himself,
But the hangman's noose finished the
lovebird."

All the while she spoke
I trembled and stared at my girl
I call her that, because by this time
I loved her every curve and curl

I had to possess the photograph
And make her my very own
"Is it for sale, this pic of the girl?"
The dread that it wasn't sat like a stone

"No, I'm sorry, it's not."
The waitress had a scowl on her face
"You really should move away from that
wall
Your love of her will only end in disgrace."

"You're right, of course, I'm sorry.

It's strange that I feel this way.
I'll pay the check and leave you now.
It's really been a very strange day."

I stood and walked to the counter,
Knowing that I would return.
I left the diner, stumbling and dazed.
To have that photo, I longed and yearned.

As I sat in my car and waited
For the diner to close for the night
Her eyes in the photograph burned in my
brain.
What I planned made me want to take flight.

So, finally midnight came
And the lights of the diner went out
I watched awhile, my heart pounding loud
I waited until there was no-one about.

Then I crept to the back of the building
And forced a window to open.
I climbed inside, it was quiet and dark.
There was no-one left, as I had hoped

Once inside, I saw it.
On the wall and lit by the moon.
Her beauty, it called me, I tip-toed near
And knew I would possess her soon.

I had the photo in my hands.
What I felt, it left me in tears.
All of my life, I've wanted a woman

To call my 'my love' for the rest of my
years.

Suddenly, the lights flashed on
And the waitress was shaking her head.
"I told you to stay away from that photo.
Now leave, or this gun will make sure you
are dead."

I stared at the waitress a moment,
Then at the photo in my hand.
"I'm not leaving here without this picture,"
And with that, I hit the waitress a backhand.

As she fell, she fired the gun.
It missed, so I kicked and I hit
Until she was still, with blood on the floor.
With dread and fear, I bent and was sick.

I looked, then, at the photo
And got a terrible shock.
My Marilyn smiled, but not at all sweet.
Her grin was malicious, and her eyes, they
did mock.

Her dressed was soaked with blood,
The photo hadn't shown any there.
And in her hand, she held a gun
Pointed at me, I would swear.

I grabbed the gun the waitress had fired
And broke down the door at the back.
I found the sheriff waiting for me,

A shotgun waiting to attack.

I dropped the gun and the photo
And let him arrest me instead.
The police car was cold, the jail cell was
worse
And all the while, Marilyn's photo filled my
head.

So now, I sit here and wait.
Marilyn has left me bereft.
My life is destroyed, for the love of a photo.
Lethal injection is all I have left.

Money Urned

It was a day of searching
In thrift stores, far and wide
I had my eyes on finding
A treasure, beauty to be spied

Most of what I found
Was ugly, useless junk
Trash that no-one wanted
Broken stuff and clothes that stunk

Then, I stepped into a store
It smelled of incense and perfumes
A light and pleasant atmosphere
With neat and tidy rooms

I waved polite 'Hello'
to the lady behind a desk

She smiled and said "Come in.
You're welcome. I'm simply taking a rest."

I started to look around me
I poked and I peeked on the shelves
I found some wonderful items to buy
I never guessed one would send me to hell

Silverware, cups and saucers,
Jewelry, tattered, old dolls
Wooden boxes that played tinny tunes
Nice lace and gossamer scarve

A lot of the items I saw
Would look beautiful in my home
And so, I started to gather some things
To decorate where I lived alone

Then, in one darkened corner
Hidden from the light of the sun
A single shelf held a vase
Made of bronze, with a name on a plate
The thing was clearly an urn

I picked it up, it felt heavy
I couldn't read the engraved name
So I carried it to the owner
She looked at me with shock and shame

"I'd forgotten about this item.
Inside are the ashes of one
Who lived his life like a saintly man.
He was charitable, handsome and calm.

Walking home one night
Some men chose to kill him and steal
His money and watch, all that he had
In here are his ashes sealed."

As she spoke, the urn moved
I felt it tremble and shake
"Why does it shiver, here in my hands?"
My voice began to quake

"It isn't dear, it simply can't.
It's just a burial vase."
I bought it along with all of the rest
Then I waved 'goodbye' to her place

All the drive home, I was nervous
I couldn't tell why I was scared
The items I'd gotten were harmless enough
But, still, my nerves were thread-bare

I got to my door and locked it
My breathing was shallow and quick
I went upstairs and lay on the bed
The air in the house was heavy and thick

I tried to calm my heart
Which pounded my chest with pain
Confused and alone, I started to sweat
Something was here, it was plain

Then, from downstairs, I terrible crash
Terror held me in its grip

I stood and crossed to the door on tip-toe
What I heard caused my sanity to slip

Coming up the stairs towards the hall
Footsteps, steady and measured and slow
The front door was locked, the windows too
Outside, it had started to snow

I called out, "Who is down there?"
No-one answered my cry
The footsteps came nearer, I waited to see
Someone had gotten inside

Then, the footfalls ceased
I waited, my heartbeats were dread
Tears filled my eyes, I started to cry
An aching pounded my head

A shock hit my body like lightening
I froze and started to swoon
A hand gripped my throat, another, my arm
With a shove, I started to move

I was pushed down the stairs, I moved
slowly
My legs were weak and unsure
I got to the living room and looked around
The first thing I saw was the urn

It lay on the ground in pieces
Footprints, in ash, on the rug
"That was my home for years," said a voice
My dizziness felt like a drug

"I was a good man. My life
Was helpful and kind to others.
But then an attack left me for dead
For hours I lay and suffered

"My name, when alive, was Tim Atkins.
I preached at a church far from here.
I cared and I gave. That all changed
The night I learned pain and fear.

Now that I'm free, I'll repay
Everyone for the day that I died.
I'll kill and I'll steal and get rich in the deal.
I'll earn my life back with fear."

His hand squeezed my throat till I gagged
The room started to turn black
The last thing I heard, before my heart
stopped
Was laughter from the man at my back

Prison Switch

He worked as a guard in a prison
He was big and strong and tough
He wasn't afraid of anyone there
He could handle them when it got rough

The warden gave him a job
In a wing for the worst of the worst
All of the prisoners cared about no-one
All they wanted was to kill and to hurt

He took the job and was proud
He could prove to his wife and their kids
That all of these bad men would do as he
said
He told them what to do and they did

Then, one day, they brought in
A man they call a murder mark
All he wanted was to eat and to kill
He prowled the world like a shark

The shark had been scheduled for death
Execution would name his fate
The world would be rid of all that he was
Anger and fear and consuming hate

The guard met the shark in his cell
And laughed at the beast without shame
The shark became angrier, day by day
Revenge would be his, when it came

The shark's execution was hastened
No appeal was ever made
The shark would not sit on death-row for
years
His death was only weeks away

The guard spent all of his time
Ridiculing the shark in his cell
Everything that the guard said
Was meant to tear the beast apart

Jokes and insults, frightening threats
There was nothing the guard left unsaid
The beast took all that the guard said
Into the darkest place in his head

The guard went home the night before
The execution was to take place
He smiled with pride and boasted to
His wife about the shark's disgrace

The guard fell asleep, and when he awoke
He knew that something was wrong
A leather hood made breathing hard
His arms and legs were fettered strong

He was lying on his back
With needles in each arm
He could hear some voices near
He listened with increased alarm

The guard was frightened suddenly
As he struggled to get up
He felt weaker, as time passed
He wanted answers quick enough

Then a voice spoke in his ear
He knew the quiet sound
Of the shark, the guttural voice
The guard lay still in his dumbfound

"I know a woman," the beast intoned
"who cast a spell, you see.
She came to visit, while I waited

And wished that you could become me."

"She owed me for a past favor,
For killing a man she loved
Who met another woman and
He gave to her his love."

"The witch repaid her debt to me
By brewing up a spell.
When it was done, my time had come
To send your joking soul to hell.

"Now, I am you and you are me.
You are the beast, you see.
And when you're dead, I'll see your wife
To have whatever fun I please."

The guard, he tried to scream, just then
But, to no avail
The deadly chemicals began to course
Throughout his veins, and leave him frail

And, as he died, the guard shed tears
He knew that he was beaten
His heart, it stopped, his soul, it burned
He knew the beast had gotten even

John O'lantern

The people of the tiny town
They all had heard the tale
Of John de Magnus, business man
Whose final venture failed

He lost his money and his home
His wife and children left
John's reputation suffered most
And left his life bereft

He drank and smoked and took bad drugs,
A whirlpool of depression
Instead of finding his way back,
he missed a priceless lesson

He chose a frightened coward's way out
And all the world he blamed
So, late one night, he lit a fire
And his life burst into flames

He doused himself in gasoline
And lit a match he held
He lay down in a pumpkin patch
And knew the suffering of hell

For years, his story has been told
By those who lived close to
The place of John's last shrieking
And has become a Halloween 'boo'

The story goes, the ghost of John
Wreaks havoc, late at night
He captures someone in the town
And sets their clothes alight

Now, in the town, there is a man
A banker and a cad

He likes to pick on all the folks
And he laughs when they feel bad

He's stolen money from the bank
And never has been caught
He's foreclosed othe people's homes
And left in the street to rot

He's never had a date, you see
To women, he can't be trusted
'cause when he talks to anyone
They walk away disgusted

And so, one night, the banker
Drove to a town nearby
And searched for a woman all alone
To grab her, take her and make her cry

In his plan, he succeeded
He knew the woman he killed
He dumped her body and drove back home
His heart, it raced with the thrill

No-one missed her right away
So he planned another
A trip to find someone else
To catch and take and smother

Several times, the banker drove
To find his fix of fun
He stood much straighter, felt much stronger
And knew his power had just begun

All the time the banker killed
Hi town, it grieved and trembled
Would the murderer come there?
And so, the town assembled

They cried "Let's find this monster now.
We have to stop his killing stint.
Let's catch him, try him and find him guilty.
Then, we'll tear him, limb from limb."

And, all the time they plotted
The bank knew full well
They'd never catch him at his game
No matter how much they screamed and
yelled

Months passed slow, in agony
The summer turned to Fall
The police, they couldn't find a clue
Their investigation stalled

The year, it slowly turned to dusk
The leaves they changed their color
Red and orange, green and brown
This was an October like no other

Halloween is spooky time
Pumpkins lit, decorations hung
The night came on in calm, warm breezes
The kids were ready for party fun

The banker wanted kids to come
And visit his house for candy
So, he put up paper frights

And made his house look 'dandy'

He sat upon his creaking porch
And waited to hand out goodies
He wore a pumpkin mask and suit
And said, "Kids, come and have some
cookies."

But, out of all of those who passed
There was just one person who stopped
A man approached, shook the banker's hand
And said, "You've never been on top."

"My name is John de Magnus.
I died here, years ago.
This is my town, I built it up.
And now, it's time for you to go."

And then, the ghost of John de Magnus
Touched the mask the banker wore
And with a spark and a scream
An explosion blasted apart the porch

And now, the terror is no more
The town can breathe relief
At least until John de Magnus
Decides to change that vain belief

You Can't Go Back

Growing up in a small town
My favorite toy was 'Buster, Space Ranger'
His plastic helmet kept him safe
His laser guns stopped all danger

My mother gave him to me one Christmas

She said, "You'll fly in space, my boy.
Just like Buster, you'll see the stars."
And so, Buster became my favorite toy

He went with me everywhere
I took him to the local pool
I carried him to my friends' for play
He went, every day, with me, to school

I gripped his chubby spacesuit in my hands
And dreamt of racing to the stars
He took me from my earthly fears
To other worlds, we rocketed far

As I grew, I left him home
In my room, propped on a shelf
My life moved on, I made my way
To a smarter, older self

I slowly left him in my past
I found a talent, while in school
Science helped me think and dream
In research and Astronomy, too

I married and had two children
And found a job which led
To work in astrophysics
And put space travel into my head

As time went by, I found a way
To a spot on a rocket ship
As a mission specialist
Gathering data on this trip

Five of us were seated
In a new spaceship

The lifters fired and shot us up
Into the vacuum we rode

Each of us had our duties
Mine was mathematical analysis
I gathered the numbers and formed
conclusions
And sent them to Earth with a button click

And then one day, it happened
A nitrotank began to leak
My sight became blurry, my sight became
slurred
My muscles were pain-filled and weak

I searched for the other astronauts
My companions had already died
I managed to put on and atmosphere suit
And gulped in air, once inside

An explosion rocked throughout the ship
Not far from my means of escape
I looked outside a view portal
To watch the escape pod detonate

All contact with Earth is lost
I am stranded, here, alone
Explosions are tearing the ship apart
In my grief and panic, I think of home

The thought that strikes me last
While I burn in flames, as in hell
Is the toy rocket man I had as a child
My 'Buddy' I played with and loved so well

Egypt Beckons

I call my queen, Suhkenaaten,
"My wife, bring me some beer."
I gather my children, princes and princesses
To make certain my family is safe and near

My kingdom spreads before me
The Nile, I see, is flowing slow
Artisans, farmers, pyramid slaves
All pay their respects, as my power grows

A priest hands me a papyrus
I issue an edict to state
A holiday planned to honor myself
With food and wine, honey and dates

My subjects line up with gifts
For me, my queen and my wards
I order my guards to bring my chariot
And ready my armies for war

My men and I thunder onward
Pounding the ground into dust
With arrows and spears, daggers and swords
We decimate all, as we must

And then, a funeral procession
Sends my first-born on his way
To life on the plain of afterlife glory
A pall of grief darkens the day

I then call my slaves to my bedchamber
And drown my tears in sweat
With pleasure of all I desire to taste
The pain of the day disappears on my bed

And then, all at once, pain grips me
I open my eyes to my queen
A furious look disfigures her face
She uses a blade to vent her spleen

"I tire of you, my Pharoah.
Your war cost me my son.
I send you to flames to burn for my loss.
You'll live eternity loved by no-one."

Then, darkness comes and I hear a voice
Calling a name that I know
Suddenly slammed by heat and agony
I snap back to myself dying slow

The time is now present-day
I'm wearing jeans and a shirt
I'm lying on rocks, covered in dust
My bones are broken, my organs are burst

It started this morning, on a tour
My wife and I are in Egypt
A vacation to see the pyramids of yore
And the Sphinx and tombs on our trip

While touring a burial cave
I ignored the guard's caveat
"Don't stray away, stay with me.
This place is dangerous if you wander off."

But, I walked into a side-passage
The ground disappeared beneath my feet
I plummeted far and landed hard
My cries for help were barely a squeak

And now, as I die, I lay dreaming

My imagination makes me a king
An ancient pharaoh, centuries past
Being murdered in hate by my vindictive
queen

Now, the dream is gone and I'm fading
My blood coats the ground, thick and red
My legs are shattered, my back is split
And my skull is in pieces in my head

So, my consciousness fades
I hear my wife as she yells
I'm certain I felt her hand on my back
And she pushed, just before I fell

Unidentified frightening Object

We were flying high above
A desert far below
Our twin-prop airplane buzzed along
A thunderstorm in tow

The lightening flashed close to us
Thunder shook the plane
Wind, it rocked us back and forth
Our view, obscured by rain

I radioed for help to find
A place where we could land
An airport close nearby
A landing strip near to hand

Static was our only answer
No-one heard our call
I now was guided by my wits
To keep us from an engine stall

Then, from far behind the plane
A spotlight shown around us
The clouds lit up, the cockpit too
We did not know where the other craft was

All of a sudden, the plane became still
We stopped all forward motion
The storm, it raged all around the plane
But we swayed as on an ocean

The spotlight grew and the air became hot
The four of us sat in silence
We couldn't see, we became light-blind
We became terrified and tense

The plane was dead, the propellers still
The gauges all read at 'zero'
Then we heard a pounding sound
That slammed us above and below

My wife sat beside me, starting to cry
Our friends were silent and searching
I slipped slowly into a dread
Made worse when the plane started lurching

We were surrounded, in a blink of an eye
By screeching metal and shattering glass
We all started screaming, it all seemed
unreal
How long would this sound of hell last?

And then, we floated into the air
The plane was no longer in sight
We became one with the light and sound
I saw no-one, not my friends nor my wife

The nerves of my body began to burn
Without flames, my body was on fire
Light and pain, I knew nothing else
Had the plane crashed and had I expired

But no, I still lived, this now was proved
As the light faded slowly away
I found myself lying on a table in straps
And staring at creatures, what they were, I
can't say

And so, it began, and unending agony
Of machines and chemicals and screams
My mind went away and left me a blank
No more thoughts or life or dreams

I don't know how long it's been going on
I know nothing of life anymore
The creatures who took me have left me
bereft
Of my mind and my life of before

Long and willowy, gray and smooth
These things never speak to me
They come and go, never making a sound
Where I was, I couldn't see

And now I'm alone, in pain and afraid
I don't know when or if it will end
I can't even wonder to myself self anymore
What became of my wife and my friends

The Hound

A new play by
William Armstrong
Based on the classic story
By H. P. Lovecraft

Setting: The sitting room of Blackthorne Manor. A couch is
C. A coffee table is D.C. A desk, piled with books is L. A
large curtained window is L. A curtained window is U.C. A
bookshelf is R. This bookshelf opens to the basement. The
front door is U.C. A doorway is U. R. Arcane tomes line
the bookshelves.
Time: Early 20ᵗʰ century.

<u>SCENE 1</u>

(ST. JOHN and BLACKTHORNE sit on the couch C. St.
John holds a six inch long bone marked with symbols.)

ST. JOHN
This is one of our best finds yet. Early eighteenth century,
judging by the markings. Those are strange, though. I
haven't seen any like these before. They're like tattoo
hammer strikes. You know, someone uses a rock and a
fashioned stick to pound ink into a person.

BLACKTHORNE
Sounds painful. But, I'm sorry to disappoint you, my
friend. Those aren't tattoo strikes. They're teeth marks.
That bone is probably from some poor soul who was
captured by a tribe of cannibals.

ST.JOHN

Oh, my god. That's disgusting. Chewed to the marrow, by the looks of it. We should find a special niche for this one. I can almost feel an aura of fear emanating from it.

BLACKTHORNE

Probably some residual energy left over from the victim's last few moments on the dining table. Let's not be too superstitious. We'll research the area a little more, first. Find out if there were, in fact, cannibals, at any point in time, indigenous to the region.

ST. JOHN

Solid thinking. I like these strange glyphs. They're ornamental, almost as if it was used in rituals. They're marked using red paint.

BLACKTHORNE

You're wrong again. That's not paint. It's blood. And, see this hole drilled at the top. I would guess it was used as a necklace.

ST. JOHN

Incredible. Well, since we found it near an ancient fire pit, your surmise is probably correct. Cannibals.

BLACKTHORNE

(Blackthorne retrieves a large book from the desk L.)

See here. In Thurston's book. He traveled in that region in the mid- eighteen hundreds. It says here, there was a lot of native activity, at one time, where we found that bone. People going in to subdue and subjugate the locals. Probably wanting free labor. But, there were frequent uprisings.

ST. JOHN
I guess the natives didn't like the idea of stitching clothes for no money.

BLACKTHORNE
He also says they used witchcraft.

ST. JOHN
Who didn't in those days? Black magic to waylay a victim and lure them to their demise, and cannibalism to absorb a person's energy by partaking in their flesh. People after my own heart.

BLACKTHORNE
You don't have the stomach, or the balls, to eat another human being.

ST. JOHN
Gloria might disagree with you about that. But, you're probably right. My stomach churns if my steak is even a little under-cooked.

BLACKTHORNE
My point exactly. And, look at this. Thurston talks about a corpse-eating cult that actually developed an identifying symbol.

ST. JOHN
What does he mean by that?

BLACKTHORNE
Smaller tribes usually stuck together; ate together, hunted together, etc. They knew every other member of the tribe. But, larger clans were generally more spread out. Since they covered more ground, there had to be a way to know who to keep away from the group. Larger tribes developed

identifying symbols, so they would know one another. (Blackthorne points to the bone.) Look at this.

ST, JOHN
It's small, kind of hard to see. But, it looks like an Ibex, but with wings. Why would they use something that looks like a hound with wings as their symbol?

BLACKTHORNE
I don't know. Perhaps it symbolized their notion of swift justice.

ST. JOHN
Swift justice?

BLACKTHORNE
You know, swift retribution; quick retaliation. They certainly had their hands full, trying to stay free of those wanting to enslave them. I think you're right, though. It does resemble a dog with wings.

ST. JOHN
Wait a minute! A flying hound. That sounds familiar. I think we've seen this before. Wait here. I'll be right back. (St. John moves to the bookshelf R. He activates a switch and opens the bookshelf. He disappears inside, then reappears holding a green jade amulet.)

BLACKTHORNE
What have you got?

ST. JOHN
Do you remember where we found this?

BLACKTHORNE

We dug it up in a Holland graveyard. It was in a coffin. The person buried there was a grave-robber.

ST. JOHN
Ironic, don't you think? I'm sure whoever was buried in the coffin with this amulet would see the funny side of being dug up by grave-robbers.

BLACKTHORNE
No doubt. And, I think you're right. The symbol on the bone, and this amulet, bear a striking resemblance. The dog-shaped head, the wings, and both representations show claws and fangs. They're definitely from the same tribe.

ST. JOHN
Not necessarily. It's a well-documented fact that different cultures have begun at approximately the same time, relatively speaking, then developed along similar lines, guided by survival needs and their environment.

BLACKTHORNE
The amulet has flecks of dried blood on it as well. A little more than co-incidentally, I think. Obviously, this particular group of corpse-eaters was wide- spread. The amulet, we found in Holland, and the bone, in South America.

ST. JOHN
So, the person buried with the amulet was a traveler. He no doubt acquired it during his time abroad. I mean, look how far we traveled to find these two items. He was, no doubt, a like-minded soul.

BLACKTHORNE
You know, St. John, you have a way of taking the spark out of a notion.

ST. JOHN

Not at all. There's still blood on both items. A little more research to uncover the truth, and we might actually have a publishable theory.

BLACKTHORNE

I don't think we need scientific types and newspaper reporters seeking us out for information and stumbling on our hidden secret. That cellar, if found, would mean lock-up for life. Besides, something down there is beginning to smell.

ST. JOHN

I'll look into it. But, you do make a good point.

BLACKTHORNE

Before we do anything else, we need to add this to our catalog.

ST. JOHN

Alright. I'll return the amulet to its pedestal, and find a suitable niche for that.
(Both exit into the cellar.)

SCENE 2

Setting: Basement.
Time: Same day.

(ST. JOHN and BLACKTHORNE enter L. into the basement. It is crowded with shelves crammed with stolen grave artifacts, jewelry, books and paintings. Two chairs are C. L.)

ST. JOHN

You're right. Something stinks. Perhaps one of our illegally obtained taxidermy trophies. I'll go see. (St. John exits R. then returns holding an adult male, stuffed head.) This is it. The eye socket is moldering. I'll dispose of it when we go upstairs.

BLACKTHORNE

Alright. So, how many artifacts have we collected so far? I'm guessing almost three thousand, to date.

ST. JOHN

An accurate guess. Two thousand, eight hundred and seventy-four. You know, it always makes me laugh, when you refer to all of this individually as 'artifacts'. It makes us sound like legitimate archeologists.

BLACKTHORNE

What's the difference? Most of the world's great collections, privately owned or in museums, started out as items raided from tombs. Even items scavenged from ship-wrecks, technically, belong to someone else.

ST. JOHN

True. But, they aren't actually pieces of someone else. I think the government would have a difficult job viewing our collection as a legitimate collection.

(St. John lights a cigarette from a cigarette lighter attached to a stuffed, human hand.)

BLACKTHORNE

Why did you make that?

ST. JOHN

I needed something to light my cigarettes with. But, the rest of the collection is just as we found it. Beautiful, aren't they? Books revering denizens living among brimstone and fire. A small fortune of trinkets stolen from graves all over the world.

BLACKTHORNE

Urns made centuries ago, with the ashes of their owners still inside. Gold necklaces, diamond rings and pearl earrings.

ST. JOHN

Solid silver plates, mugs and tableware.

BLACKTHORNE

Paintings by some of history's most talented and disturbed artists.

ST. JOHN

Adult skulls calcified to horrific perfection by the passing of time, and newborn heads made eternal by the embalmer's chemical touch.

BLACKTHORNE

(Blackthorne takes a very thick book off of one of the shelves). Not to mention our catalog, noting every artifact, the date of the find, and where we located it, covered in tanned, human skin. I hate to remember how much it cost.

ST. JOHN

But, worth every penny. Sometimes, I imagine I can smell the perfume the lady wore.

BLACKTHORNE

You do have an active imagination. The thought of what would happen if all this were discovered makes me think. We've added rooms to our museum, to expand it twice already. We should consider installing a door down here as well, for an easy escape, or in case of fire.

                    ST. JOHN
Very well. I'll contact a less-than-reputable contractor. Someone with more of an eye towards money than scruples.

                    BLACKTHORNE
Let's get upstairs and air the place out for the girls visit tomorrow.

                    ST. JOHN
And, I'll bury this (St. John indicates the stuffed human head.) in the garden.

                    SCENE 3

Setting: Living room.
Time: The same day.

(BLACKTHORNE and ST.JOHN are in the mansion living room. Blackthorne walks to the front door U. and PROFESSOR WADE enters.)

                    BLACKTHORNE
Please come in, Professor Wade. You remember St. John.

                    PROFESSOR WADE
Yes, from my Social Psychology class. How are you, sir?

                    ST. JOHN
I'm well, professor, thank you. Can I get you something to drink?

                    PROFESSOR WADE

Some ale would be fine, thanks.

                    ST. JOHN
Coming right up.

                PROFESSOR WADE
So, what have you boys been up to since you left school?

(Professor Wade takes the drink from St. John.)

                  BLACKTHORNE
Really? Where? And why? Neither of you appeared to me
to be the type to go adventuring abroad.

                    ST. JOHN
We've traveled just about everywhere. Touched all the
continents. It started as a quest to visit the sites of the
original seven wonders of the ancient world. You know,
broadening our minds and general view of things by seeing
new places and meeting new people.

                PROFESSOR WADE
An admirable endeavor.

                    ST. JOHN

We thought we would stop at various city capitals and
collect souvenirs of our travels.

                PROFESSOR WADE
You gentlemen don't strike me as the typical middle-class
tourist types. What was different about your travels?

                  BLACKTHORNE

Well, we remember your advice with regards exploring out of the ordinary sights. You know, trekking off the beaten path.

                    PROFESSOR WADE
Of course. You get to the root, the very heart of a place, and its people, by staying away from the typical tourist traps. They're only money-making ventures anyway.

                    BLACKTHORNE
Well, our trips slowly evolved from city site-seeing, into less cultured journeys. We found ourselves trekking into desert stretches, mangrove forests and even, for some strange reason, an expanse of frozen tundra.

                    PROFESSOR WADE
Excellent! And what finds did your forays net you?

                    ST. JOHN
Plenty. Our cultural knowledge greatly exceeds what it was before. We've made valuable friends and contacts, which have turned out to be quite useful to us. You see, we began to collect arcane artifacts.

                    PROFESSOR WADE
Arcane artifacts?

                    BLACKTHORNE
Certainly. A couple of years ago, we happened on an obscure bookseller in the Ukraine. He sold us a manuscript pertaining to the sacrificial rites of the South American Olmecs. Our Meso-American sojourn to investigate its claims led us to a scholar who was keen to buy the manuscript. We sold it, and made enough money to buy our next unique find, the journal of a ghost-hunter who disappeared in China, while investigating a violent spirit

infestation in one of their temples. We kept that journal for ourselves, but found that there are unusual items, which collectors will pay substantial sums of money for, all over the globe.

ST. JOHN

What started out as a hobby, just for our enjoyment, and to make a little profit for ourselves, has turned into a full-fledged occupation.

PROFESSOR WADE

So, where are the items you've kept? May I see them?

BLACKTHORNE

We've actually kept very few. Most of them we've gotten rid of for the money. But, we do have a few really interesting artifacts. Why don't you show the professor, St. John?

ST. JOHN

My pleasure. (St. John retrieves the bone and jade amulets from the desk L.) We believe this to be part of a necklace, worn by a cult in Guyana. We're guessing it's approximately four thousand years old.

PROFESSOR WADE

Hmm. Teeth marks on it. And, it's what has been called a 'blood relic', meaning it was probably used in sacrificial ceremonies. Incredible.

BLACKTHORNE

And, see on its base. A mark resembling a canine with wings.

PROFESSOR WADE

Oh my god, you're right.

ST. JOHN

And look at this. We found this amulet in an ancient
churchyard in Holland. You see, it appears to be the same
figure as that on the bone.

PROFESSOR WADE

It does look similar, as you say. Have you found out
anything about what this winged canine symbolizes?

BLACKTHORNE

No. We've read into Egyptian myths, because it so closely
resembles their deity Anubis, but have found nothing.

ST. JOHN

Blackthorne believes it's some sort of identifying symbol.

PROFESSOR WADE

It could be. But, I have to ask you. You said you found the
amulet in Holland. I'm sure it wasn't lying on the ground in
a graveyard. How did you come by it?

BLACKTHORNE

I'm not sure we should go into the details, Professor. You
might not approve.

ST. JOHN

Let's just say, we're fairly certain the owner won't come
looking for it anytime soon.

PROFESSOR WADE

Gentlemen, that doesn't matter to me. I'm not going to say
anything to anyone. If I understand you correctly, you're
not the first to bring long forgotten items back into the
public eye. Almost everything on display in the world's

great museums had to be dug up. Just be careful not to get caught.

BLACKTHORNE

We will. We have a few more items you might like to have a look at. Come with us to the library.

PROFESSOR WADE

Very well.

SCENE 3

Setting: The living room.
Time: The same day.

(GLORIA, TRICIA, BLACKTHORNE and ST.JOHN are arranged in the living room.)

GLORIA

So, you boys are back. Did you bring any souvenirs of your travels?

ST. JOHN

If you're asking if we brought you any presents, yes, we did.

BLACKTHORNE

We'll pass out gifts later. So, what have you two been up to?

TRICIA

Waiting breathlessly for your return.

GLORIA

Seriously, I've been completing my master's concerto. One hundred and thirty-seven pages of sublime melody and richly layered brilliance.

ST. JOHN
I've always loved you for your self-effacing modesty.

GLORIA
Why pretend I'm not going to be the next Dvorak? The
world deserves my music and I deserve its adulation.

BLACKTHORNE
And you? Why Mozart here has been turning the music
world on its head, what have you been doing?

TRICIA
Languishing in tedium. Professor Lindstrom has his
graduate students preparing research notes on cultural
statistics.

BLACKTHORNE
And, what do your numbers quantify?

TRICIA
How long I'll last in his class before my head explodes
from sheer boredom. I'm not kidding you, the man can take
a subject that could be interesting and illuminating, and
cause an entire classroom to want to mutiny.

BLACKTHORNE
Hang in there, girl. I'm sure it will get better. You just need
to tie the subject matter in with the rest of your classes.

ST. JOHN
All courses are boring in and of themselves. The trick is to
see their purpose beyond just the hour or so of instruction.

BLACKTHORNE
Besides, you'll top the class in results, I'm sure.

TRICIA

I'm confident I will. It's only that the malaise, the mind-numbing, soul-deadening ennui, has taken hold, and threatens to overwhelm me. If I don't find something stimulating soon, I'll quit school and become a gypsy.

ST. JOHN

Don't do that. The gypsy life is notoriously devoid of opportunities to shop at Harrods.

TRICIA

Trust you to appeal to the soulless consumerism in me. Fine, I'll think twice about staying in school.

GLORIA

And, if you get too bored, you can always take up grave-robbing to spice things up.

BLACKTHORNE\ ST. JOHN

What?!

BLACKTHORNE

Don't talk like that, Gloria. Who would do such a thing, simply to relieve boredom? I mean, what sort of monsters would you have to be to desecrate holy ground, just to satisfy your morbid curiosity and add spice to staid existence? The idea's ridiculous.

ST. JOHN

Completely. It's unthinkable.

GLORIA

There's been talk in the local newspapers of tomb-raiders across the country. They think it's only two or three people stealing from graveyards.

(The baying of the HOUND is heard for the first time, distantly, off L. At the same time, the lights dim slightly, then brighten. All look towards the sound.)

TRICIA
Did you bring back a dog with you?

BLACKTHORNE
No, of course not.

ST. JOHN
It belongs to one of the neighbors, no doubt. It sounded far away.

TRICIA
There aren't any neighbors close by, are there?

BLACKTHORNE
No. The closest is almost a mile away.

(The baying is heard, this time from off R. Cast looks in that direction. The lights dim, then brighten.)

ST. JOHN
Maybe it's a wandering pack. I'll go check.

BLACKTHORNE
I'll go with you. You girls stay here.

(Both men retrieve revolvers from the desk, then exit through the front door, up, R.)

GLORIA

They make too much fuss over nothing. It's just a dog.
Probably a hunting hound that got loose.

TRICIA

No doubt, you're right. This place needs a good airing. The
mustiness smells too strong from their old, rotting books.

GLORIA

Especially over here. And, it doesn't smell like musty
books. It smells, I don't know, thicker.

TRICIA

Oh my god, you're right. And, do you feel cold air coming
from around this bookcase.

(Without answering, Gloria finds and pulls the latch,
opening the bookcase. Both react to a strong, repugnant
smell.)

GLORIA

What the hell is this? Did you know this was here?

TRICIA

No, I did not. God, that smell is terrible. How can they live
with it?

GLORIA

So, let's go down and look.

TRICIA

No, I think we should wait for the men to return.

GLORIA

Don't be so afraid. Apart from the odor, how terrible can it
be?

(They link arms and descend into the cellar. After a beat, the baying of the hound is heard, followed by a high-pitched scream from the cellar.)

SCENE 4

Setting: The living room.
Time: The same day.

(TRICIA is collapsed on the couch. BLACKTHORNE administers to her. GLORIA and ST. JOHN stand together, L., examining a skull.)

TRICIA
I can't believe what I saw down there. What have you two been doing?

GLORIA
Oh, Tricia, stop behaving so girlishly. There are some wonderful items down there. This skull, for instance. Holding this, I feel like the gravedigger in Hamlet. "Poor Yorick, I knew him well."

TRICIA
Keep that away from me. It's disgusting and depraved.

GLORIA
Why? The person is dead. What's your concern?

ST. JOHN
Skulls aren't all we have found over the years, Tricia. We've found far more valuable items to add to the collection.

GLORIA

Really? Valuable? Like what?

                    ST. JOHN
I'd be more than happy to show you.

                    BLACKTHORNE
Do you two mind? I think we owe the girls some
explanation, St. John. Here, dear, drink this. It will revive
you.

                    ST. JOHN
I suppose you're right. It stems from something you
mentioned before- boredom. A need to keep life interesting.

                    BLACKTHORNE
After we finished school, we needed something to fill our
time until we began to work.

                    ST. JOHN
So, we started to collected antique items of an unusual
nature.

                    BLACKTHORNE
We found that there are collectors who will pay good
money, real money, for items with properties or themes that
most people find objectionable.

                    ST. JOHN
So, as time passed, we found we had a talent for procuring
such items and selling them off. We livened up our dull
days, and made ourselves money to live on and pay for our
various trips abroad.

                    TRICIA
So, why do you have so many? And on display?

BLACKTHORNE

As time went on, we found ourselves appreciating the object d'art we had recovered. An appreciation we hadn't expected or counted on.

TRICIA

You boys need to stop. You're justifying something ghoulish. Not only is your little 'hobby' illegal, it's immoral. You're taking things that meant something to the people they belonged to. Not to mention the memories precious to their families. It's terrible.

GLORIA

It's not as awful as all that, Tricia. Let's look at this realistically. Chances are, the things they've taken won't be missed. And, someone's enjoying them. I admit, though, the body parts are a little over the line.

ST. JOHN

We might have gotten a little carried away, but each one has a story.

TRICIA

It's wrong. And dangerous.

(The front door Up, R. shakes as something strikes it from outside.)

GLORIA

What was that?

BLACKTHORNE

I'll look.

(Blackthorne opens the front door, then holds up a large, dead bat.)

BLACKTHORNE
It's a bat. It's dead. And huge.

TRICIA
Just toss it away and come back inside.

GLORIA
I want to see more of your 'museum'.

TRICIA
I'll wait up here.

BLACKTHORNE
I'll wait up here with you.

TRICIA
No. You should go with them. I'm just going to lie here.

(A series of loud 'thumps' sound at the front door and windows UC. and L. Blackthorne and St. John look out through the curtains.)

ST. JOHN
Oh my god. Bats are pounding the house. There's a cloud of the things.

BLACKTHORNE
Hundreds, possibly thousands, of them. I've never seen anything like it. They're flying kamikaze into the house.

TRICIA
Maybe they're attracted to the light, the same moths are.

(A baying of the hound is heard off R.)

ST. JOHN

They're leaving.

BLACKTHORNE

They're flying in the direction of the howling. I think you girls should leave. Something's going on, and I don't want you here for whatever it is.

ST. JOHN

I'll walk them out to their carriage.

BLACKTHORNE

Take you revolver, just in case.

TRICIA

This is ridiculous. We're just as safe here with you as we would be at home.

GLORIA

Besides, I want to know what is happening.

BLACKTHORNE

If it's what I think it is, you need to leave now. I'll explain later. Come back as quickly as you can, St. John. We may need to fortify the place.

ST. JOHN

What are you thinking?

BLACKTHORNE

Get them on their way home. I need a minute to think.

(St. John, Tricia and Gloria exit through the front door. Blackthorne sits at a writing desk and begins narrating as he writes.)

BLACKTHORNE

A strange occurrence has begun to assail us. Since discovering a link between the ceremonial bone and the amulet we believe is symbolic of a cult of cannibals, we have heard the unceasing bay of a hound in the distance. My imagination has left me believing the sound is growing closer. And, tonight the house was the site of a further phenomenon. An attack of the type I've only read about in stories. I believe there is a connection, and I fear for our safety.

(St. John enters through the front door.)

ST. JOHN

The girls got away. Their horse bolted as soon as they were seated. The house is engulfed in a cloud of those flying rats. And, that's not all...

(A crash of splintering wood is heard from deep within the cellar. Both men stare down inside.)

SCENE 5

Setting: The basement.
Time: Same day.

(The lights rise on BLACKTHORNE and ST. JOHN in the cellar, looking off L.)

ST. JOHN

That crash definitely came from deeper in the cellar. You be the first.

BLACKTHORNE

Look, we don't want whatever is down there to get into the
house. It's obviously coming in our direction. We wait
here, and meet it with our guns blasting it to pieces. It's our
best chance.

ST. JOHN

No, our best chance is to flee the house and bolt in our own
carriage.

BLACKTHORNE

It found us here, probably because of that damned amulet.
It'll find us anywhere.

ST. JOHN

Then let's set the place ablaze and leave, destroying the
amulet and that, whatever-it-is, in the process.

BLACKTHORNE

My family has lived here for generations, St. John. I'm not
going to become homeless by destroying it! Here, take this
sword. (Blackthorne removes a sword from a shelf.) If we
run out of bullets, we'll meet it with our own claws.

(The HOUND roars from off L.)

ST. JOHN

It sounds monstrous. It has the roar of a lion. Look, if it
destroyed that door we installed, then its flesh and blood.
I'm going to meet it half-way. You stay here. I'm going
down there.

BLACKTHORNE

No, you not. (ST. JOHN dashes off stage, L.) Come back
here, you idiot!

(The sounds of tremendous roaring and howling are mixed with St. John's screams.)

BLACKTHORNE

St. John!?

(The screams cease and snarling is heard to be growing in volume, off L, Blackthorne finally sees the hound, but the hound is not seen by the audience.)

BLACKTHORNE

Oh dear god!

(A loud roar is heard off, L. Blackthorne fires in the direction of the sound, then exits through the cellar entrance.)

SCENE 6

Setting: The living room.
Time: the same day.

(The lights rise on BLACKTHORNE entering R. from the cellar. He slams the bookcase entrance shut, holding it closed, while the hound, unseen, slams its bulk against the bookcase, emitting deafening howls and roars. Blackthorne is thrown back. The bookcase crashes open, and the hound, still unseen, roars.)

BLACKTHORNE

 St. John was you're sacrifice… (The HOUND roars.)That poor soul in the coffin in which we found the amulet was your sacrifice… (The hound roars.) I will not be your sacrifice. We were wrong to intrude into your domain, but I am not yours!

(The stage lights instantly shut off. With the theatre momentarily dark, a single gun-shot is heard, followed by the hound baying. The lights slowly rise, revealing Blackthorne lying dead, Down C.)

Curtain

www.ingramcontent.com/pod-product-compliance
Lightning Source LLC
Chambersburg PA
CBHW060714030426
42337CB00017B/2874